my cool campervan.

my cool campervan.

an inspirational guide to retro-style campervans

jane field-lewis + **chris haddon**

photography by **tina hillier**

PAVILION

contents

introduction

When people think of campervans they almost always recall the iconic VW T2, that familiar, happy-faced, slow-moving van that embodies the virtues of enjoying the journey, of taking your time and inevitably stopping to enjoy the glory of a roadside cup of tea. However, there is a world of forgotten campervans out there: the iconic Bedford CA, the classic Commer, the vintage Dodge, the converted Citroën H Van, the big American RV and an idiosyncratic world of individual conversions to campers.

Writing the sister book to *My Cool Caravan* gave me, my co-author Chris, and Tina Hillier, our talented photographer, the chance to shoot these vans, some unique, some commonplace, but all treasured by their owners, who embrace campervan life to the full.

We set off on a 3500-mile trip to locate the campervans and their proud owners, who shared their memories of family holidays under candy-striped pop-top roofs, of ice creams on long road trips, of sunny days and simple pleasures.

Spending time on the road we experienced again the joys of outdoor life, idle conversations, map reading and stumbling upon delightful new places – and confronting those difficult decisions: do we stop and savour the view or tear on through?

We began our trip in midsummer and with military precision. Our planning was meticulous (spreadsheets, satnav, schedules and a full-on itinerary logged into my Blackberry). All very high tech. As the seasons changed (and minus the satnav, lost on the way), we began to savour the simpler way. The pleasure of mixing serious discussion with funny and meaningless chat, the unexpectedly delicious improvised lunches, our perfectly customized picnic kit – and with notebooks and cameras, we were completely set up for life on the road. Without searching for it, the campervan lifestyle had found us.

What our journey revealed was a succession of delightful campervans, memorable locations and people happy to share their treasured memories with us. We found some classic models that had been beautifully restored, some in showroom condition despite being 30 years old, and others slightly shabby yet well-loved and well-used by people in pursuit of their hobbies, sports or the sheer pleasure of the journey itself.

A common consensus among campervan owners is the joy of being able to just set off and go, with the minimum of preparation, for a day, a weekend, or longer. A campervan offers the freedom to make a quick dash for the coast for a weekend of surfing or to a summer festival, or into the countryside for a week of walking. For some owners the campervan is the happy home for their vintage camping collection; for others it's a compact mobile art studio. But above all, these campervans celebrate individualism, style, cultural history and the great outdoors.

My Cool Campervan reveals a world beyond the stereotype, of vintage vans from another era, still loved and still on the road, of forgotten rarities, of beautifully restored mass-produced models. This book is not intended as a comprehensive guide to campervan history, but rather as a celebration of its evolving styles and designs, and the way we use our leisure time.

As a stylist I learned long ago that style is broader than fashion: these treasured campervans are beyond fashion, lovely in their own right, equipped and dressed with style, practicality and individuality.

My Cool Campervan is designed to inspire and delight, and we owe a big debt of thanks to all the contributors who have allowed us to photograph their cherished campervans.

old retro

Campervan designs began to change in the 1970s and 80s as the motor industry turned its sights towards the global market. Bodywork lost its rounded curves and became more angular and the general look of the campervans became plainer.

Wide sliding side doors replaced the old hinged panel doors, while old-fashioned chrome strips, bumpers and radiator grilles were replaced with more practical plastics. Advances in windscreen technology allowed manufacturers to let in more light by using larger areas of glass.

The relative newness of these vehicles and the availability of spare parts means that there are still plenty on the road today. They may not be as iconic as the VW T2, but they are often more spacious, more efficient and better planned than the earlier classics. And they promise just as much fun when it comes to taking to the road.

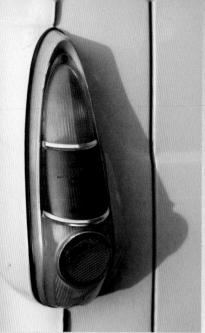

skoda

'Don't come back without it! Whatever the cost!': the exact words of Bill's wife Diana after he showed her the advert for this very unusual and rare 1992 Skoda/Taz campervan. Diana had even named the Skoda 'Daisy' before it was on their driveway.

'We don't tend to follow the masses when it comes to vehicles – the stranger the better,' comments Bill, 'quirky indulgences that we get fun out of owning.' Bill and Diana had always fancied a campervan but it took this Czechoslovakian wonder to make them take the plunge. The design has changed little since its first appearance in 1975 and much of the mechanics hark back to the cold war era.

'I guess my fascination with vehicles comes from my father. I lost contact with him when I was a child, but in my late teens, completely by chance, we became reacquainted after we found ourselves next to each other while waiting at traffic lights. From then on we spent many weekends together tinkering with engines – handy with the Skoda!'

'The Skoda's handling and ride is something to get used to – the ride is so bouncy it's rather like an amusement park ride – but we love it all the same.'

style notes

Stylistically harking back to its Eastern bloc roots, this 1992 campervan visually exudes solidity and reliability. Appearances can be deceptive – as in this case – but fortunately the owner relishes the time he has to spend tinkering with the engine and keeping up the bodywork.

The design of the interior reflects its somewhat utilitarian past in the choice of textiles and soft furnishings. The simple white cabinetry, with drilled holes instead of handles, shows a functional but stylish approach which is enjoying a resurgence in popularity today.

The driver's cabin is separated from the rest of the interior by shelves backed with wallpaper in a brown, terracotta and cream small floral design. The brown 1970s Holkham mugs, chunky storage jars and the use of wood in the interior help to create a warm, homely space while celebrating its functionality.

'We were searching the internet for a car trailer when we came across our beloved **bedford cf**
Bedford CF campervan with matching trailer,' explains Ian.

'It looked great, so we rang the number. An elderly man answered and he told us all about the Bedford. It was rather a distance to travel but well worth it. We couldn't believe how lovely it was...even better than we expected!'

'The camper was a treasured piece, in original condition with a genuine 33,000 miles on the clock. It had been owned by the gentleman from new and was much loved. He hadn't driven it since 1992 but had it serviced every year regardless. He couldn't wait to tell us about its history and the great trips he had enjoyed.'

'After two hours of chatting we finally left, but not before he kissed the camper goodbye with a tear in his eye.'

'Apart from slightly updating it we have had to do very little. The trailer is a great extra – we can arrive on site and begin to relax without unloading the van. We use a nearby campsite, so once we get in from work, we can jump in, drive off and be totally relaxed within the hour.'

style notes

This Bedford has a chubby American look, with access via a wide hinged side door, chunky chrome bumpers and a fibreglass roof that blends into the pop-top. Campervans with plenty of windows, like this one, provide a fresh, bright internal space.

The interior was originally fitted out to order and the quality of the workmanship is much appreciated by its current owner. The internal space is well considered: the sink and cooker are located opposite the side door and it is easy to move around in the camper. Adults can stand up comfortably when the large pop-top is raised.

The original curtains in a lovely lemon yellow fabric and the bright orange sink bring a touch of sunshine. Other details, such as the yellow crockery and colourful hand towels, add to that holiday feel, regardless of weather conditions.

caravelle club

'I'm a serial VW T25 owner, having had one previously for 12 years. I've always had a soft spot for vans. That, coupled with a love of the outdoors, camping and lighting fires, makes owning a camper almost obligatory.'

'There seems to be something down-to-earth about driving one of these vehicles – no pretensions – and for me there is also the element of nostalgia that can't be ignored.'

Owner Pat is part of an explosive four-piece R&B band based in Southend-on-Sea; his T25 doubles as the band's 'wagon' and is used regularly to get to gigs.

'I'm a fan of keeping vehicles looking original. Therefore I have carried out only minor interior changes, such as fitting swivelling seat bases and altering the seat configuration to allow for a full-width bed.'

The van is also used by Pat and his family for camping. 'Our daughter gets excited at the prospect of making new friends on a campsite, and as my wife's hobby is photography there are always plenty of opportunities for her to take pictures. For me, I love the excitement of preparing for a trip and hitting the road. On arrival, having found a good spot, it's awning up, cooker on, chairs out, radio on, then a splash of single malt whisky – and it has to be in that order!'

style notes

This 1987 water-cooled VW T3 (T25) was originally a day van with two rows of passenger seats. The first row of passenger seats has been removed, which provides substantial internal space for a multitude of uses.

The owner clearly has a love of nostalgia, as evidenced by the 1970s' G Plan glass-topped coffee table, goatskin rugs and the 1950s' standard lamp, which is dismantled when the van is in transit. Owner Pat likes to create the perfect chill-out environment on arrival at a campsite and with just a few items the campervan becomes part of a rock and roll lifestyle.

When required the van can adapt to a more conventional camper use by storing the retro gems at home and replacing them with equally well-chosen camping paraphernalia.

toyota devon

'Our son saw the Toyota Devon for sale nearly three years ago. Only weeks earlier we had told him that now we had retired we wanted to reignite the campervan spark which had first been lit nearly 30 years ago.' Paul and Pauline started off with a 1966 British Gas Ford Transit van converted into a camper. But as the children grew older it became impractical; reluctantly, the family found it easier to stay in guest houses. But their passion for campervans remained.

Paul continues: 'The Toyota had been owned by the same person from new for 24 years and came with the original receipt and paperwork. It was seldom slept in, by all accounts only twice, but was often seen in lay-bys with the owner reading the paper and drinking a cup of tea.'

The owner was very reluctantly selling owing to ill health. Indeed several days later he even telephoned Paul wanting to buy it back for more money – this was quickly thwarted by Pauline.

'We attend classic car shows occasionally, but it is used every week, even if we just go a few miles down the road to read the papers and relax over a cup of tea.'

style notes

When Toyota came into the campervan market it introduced well-designed, high-specification vehicles with clean lines.

This van was converted by the company Devon, which created this simple interior, still in pristine condition. The space is uncluttered, with a modern sensibility. Storage has been well thought out and is unobtrusive. Overall the feel is light and airy.

The original velour upholstery has a neat look because of its squared-off edges. The button detail and the small geometric pattern add texture to the fabric and help offset the clean lines of the hard surfaces. It isn't trying to be trendy, but looks cool and modern nevertheless.

vw t25

'With five children our caravan was bursting at the seams! A campervan would give us the space we needed, so we bought this one from new in 1982. It was also the perfect tow vehicle,' explains Reg, the original owner of this VW T25 Devon.

The combination of campervan and caravan suited Reg, his wife Diana and their children perfectly for many years, until the inevitable time in a child's life when holidaying with your parents is just not the cool thing to do. Reg continues, 'My wife and I found ourselves holidaying on our own and the VW was a luxury I was finding tricky to justify. But I just couldn't bear to part with my pride and joy.'

'I'm a window cleaner, so I came up with a plan to use it as my work van: with a few minor modifications I was able to attach my ladders. It worked out well and it also gave me somewhere warm and dry to have a cuppa and a sandwich in-between jobs.'

This continued for a few years but Reg knew deep down this was a waste of a perfectly good and very reliable camper. His friend Tony had been badgering him for months to sell the VW to him, so reluctantly Reg gave in and sold it.

'I do miss the VW, but you never know I might revert to campervan life in a few years – I might even buy it back from Tony!'

style notes

VW moved on from its iconic T2 design (see examples on pages 34, 50 and 122) with this angular, more roomy T25 (T3) with an air-cooled engine. The later T3 seen on page 20 is water-cooled and includes an additional grille above the radiator.

Of particular note here are the striking graphic lines of the striped vinyl roof and the horizontally striped red and cream bodywork.

The added touch of black is a clever technique in any design scheme. Here it is in the door handles, the stripe on the driver's door, the grille and bumpers. It 'grounds' any colour combination and works in clothing, interiors, paintings...just about anywhere.

The diagonal plaid velour upholstery is typical of the 1980s and the cream cabinetry with contrasting rounded edge doors adds to the van's confident design statement.

simple life

The well fitted, functional campervan is the obvious solution for those owners who plan to hit the road and make the most of what they have. Theirs are the campervans where styling doesn't overwhelm function, vans that are so well designed in the first place that there is nothing to add but the journey. Who doesn't want to keep things simple?

In this chapter we have a VW T2 (a second-generation van with a bay windscreen – more commonly known as Type 2 Bay) made in 1972 and still in genuine showroom condition. Then there is the modern Dutch-built Tonke packed with highly engineered and polished materials – such as sumptuous leather upholstery and a polished steel table which is hydraulically operated. Contrast that with the former Austrian draper's high-top van, much loved and slightly battered by life but providing its owner – a surgeon with a serious surfing habit – with the perfect solution to a well-balanced life.

Good design and solid usage are the hallmarks of these vehicles, campervans that let their owners follow their dreams.

vw high-top

Paul, a surgeon who lives in the beautiful Cornish coastal village of Porthtowan, doesn't just use his 1966 VW high-top on 'high days and holidays': it's also used as his daily commuting vehicle. 'It certainly breaks up the mundane rows of cars in the hospital car park,' remarks Paul.

'The VW started its life in Salzburg, Austria, as a delivery van and somehow made its way over to England and to a garage near Truro, which is where I purchased it for a very reasonable price.'

Almost every weekend the VW becomes Paul's surf wagon and changing room – perfect when changing out of wet surf clothes on a winter's day.

'I have styled the inside to resemble a vintage railway carriage and added a few mod cons for good measure. It's very spacious and comfortable to sleep in. Myself, my wife and two children, plus surfboard, have been on many trips, including a memorable tour of the west coast of Ireland.'

'I am an active member of the SAS: not the military, but 'Surfers Against Sewage' a UK-based non-profit-making organization campaigning for clean, safe recreational waters. So you will often find it parked up near a beach, bedecked in campaigning leaflets.'

Surgeons are well known for their macabre sense of humour, so Paul tracked down and added an original VW ambulance sign to the bumper. 'The VW always brings smiles and giggles to people's faces – and they do say laughter is the best medicine.'

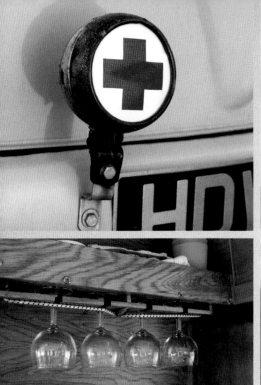

style notes

This customized commercial split-screen VW makes an interesting change from the archetypal VW campervans we are so used to seeing.

The original high-top roof was built for a draper who needed the additional height in order to hang long garments inside his delivery vehicle. Similarly the full-height barn-style doors made for easy loading and unloading of his stock. Today this extra-wide opening is ideal for getting Paul's surfboards in and out of the van. Although some wall space is lost, opening up the double doors on a summer's day makes it easy to relate the internal and external spaces.

Paul thought carefully about how best to fit out the van. His specific requirements guided the way. The interior is clad in plywood with built-in seating and storage. Safe stowage of his surfboards is addressed by custom-made slots along the roof edge of the long side of the van, with an ingenious drawstring mechanism to secure them in place.

Surf magazines are stowed in wall racks, beer and wine are stored in the cooler and drinking glasses have a bungee cord device to keep them in place and prevent breakages while on the road. All simple, clever solutions to practical problems, using low-tech methods. And nor did Paul forget to fit a good sound system!

tonke

'We had spent four years cruising the world in our beloved vintage wooden yacht, but the time came to return to dry land,' comments James. 'A campervan seemed like a good compromise, but all the campers that we'd seen were very white and plastic.'

'An article in a newspaper sparked our interest in the Tonke and it fitted the bill perfectly. The varnished mahogany interior and exterior seemed much closer to our sorely missed Royal Fifer yacht.'

'We took a trip to Holland to visit the maker and over coffee and cakes we commissioned our new Tonke. He was unfazed by our increasingly picky requests: concealed air conditioning, espresso machine, Swedish railway oil lamps, dog kennel...'

'It's a delight to drive and live in. It usually pulls a trailer containing my wife Annie's Morgan car. The main living space can be de-mounted so we can drive around in just the cab – the best of both worlds.'

'The odd thing is that the wooden construction prompts people to ask "did you make it yourself?" As a firmly hands-off DIY person this has led to some amusing exchanges.'

'One unexpected feature of the Tonke is its invisibility – particularly in France. We've parked right in the middle of busy towns without attracting comments! We suspect that people think that any moment the back will open and we'll be selling charcuterie.'

style notes

This vehicle is made to order, with the pod fitted onto a flat-bed truck. This means that it sits higher off the ground than the usual van conversions. Owners of these vehicles can choose a different pod according to their specific requirements, be these commercial or for leisure purposes. This is a modern example of how to end up with a bespoke vehicle fitted to your needs.

Here the owners' appreciation of engineering, technology and design is clear in their choice of materials.

Both the exterior and interior are mahogany lined and highly polished. This gives the van a slick, bright and sophisticated feel.

Modern design can sometimes feel a little austere. The inclusion here of an antique Swedish railway lamp and a gorgeous patchwork bedspread act as counterpoint to the brushed steel and contemporary leather finishes. These personal touches add to the integrity of the interior and can form the building blocks from which to develop the colour scheme or indeed to set the mood of the space.

citroën nomad

'I had hankered after a camper of some sort for years,' explains proud owner David. 'I had done quite a lot of camping and Continental touring in my various Citroën Dyanes from 1969 onwards, visiting Czechoslovakia, East Germany, Austria and right down to the toe of Italy.'

'I had thought longingly of a Citroën H van conversion, but living in a flat in London would make storage a major problem. I have been a member of the Citroën Car Club since 1964 and in 1999 attended their 50th Anniversary Rally. There I saw the Nomad for sale and the rest is history. I had owned a 1950 MG Y-type for 25 years, but it didn't get used that much, so I sold it and replaced it with the Nomad, which of course fits into the same small garage.'

'It didn't need restoring, just regular maintenance. There are always odd things to do to it of course, but it is not primarily a vehicle for show so it's not in *concours* condition, nor would I want it to be. It's my little snail shell – my travelling home.'

'It really does make everyone smile, even when you accumulate a substantial queue of vehicles behind you when toiling slowly up a steep hill; I have never been hooted at or received "gestures" from other drivers.'

style notes

This conversion was originally a Citroën Dyane – an upmarket version of the 2CV – and was converted by Dory, a Hampshire-based company. It displays some of the characteristic features of these vehicles, such as the classic Citroën blue, the three-bolt wheel hubs and the flat windscreen.

The van would originally have had rounded corners. These were straightened in order to add a pop-top to provide enough headroom to be able to stand up in. A fold-down pramback was added to create sufficient length in which to lie down.

It is a charming and unusual vehicle, both for its diminutive size and the ingenuity with which it has been converted. It takes just ten minutes to extend the back, put the roof up, unpack and start enjoying the great outdoors.

Alan bought the camper in 1998 and has since notched up some significant journeys, including a 4700-kilometre round trip to Alice Springs from his home in Huntly, Victoria. Although the initial credit lies with its builder, Alan was responsible for the van's restoration and the reinstatement of the period items.

'Arnold Bray left his job as a chief electrical engineer in 1951 to buy a bakery in Apollo Bay, New South Wales, Australia. Having purchased the Austin rolling chassis in 1952 he proceeded to build "Inga", his ultimate campervan. Everything he required was brought from Melbourne. The front is from an international bullnose truck, the driver and passenger doors are from an FJ Holden car and the body is constructed with aluminium sheets on aircraft framing. Arnold built the whole van, from front to back, including the ever-so-unusual boot.'

'Arnold's inaugural trip was to Tasmania in November 1959, with his wife Alma. They also toured Australia for four years, during which they encountered particularly rough roads across the Nullarbor and up past Cooktown in northern Queensland, but the Austin's tough construction held up.'

Arnold told Alan that the wrought-iron sign on the door, 'Inga', means 'rest a while' and as Alan puts it, 'That's my kinda sign.'

austin loadstar

style notes

This vehicle represents a major investment by its original owner in terms of time, technical expertise and indeed the confidence to take on such a project.

It is refreshing to look at something unique and appreciate the care and attention lavished on it. You can follow Arnold Bray's 'journey of thought' both inside and out: how the bits all fitted together, and the smooth curvy lines until you reach the boot, where surprising angles and tall tail fins almost give the impression that another car has merged into the back of it.

The motorhome originally boasted 12 electrical items: radio; TV; lights; stove; hairdryer; iron; jug; toaster; fan; vacuum; washing machine and a film projector, which was used to show slides at outback stations.

Appreciating and sympathetically restoring someone else's dream campervan, and maintaining it in order to keep it on the road, demands a certain sort of person and a good deal of commitment. Fortunately 'Inga' found in Alan just such a person.

Some campervans are produced in many thousands, but there is only one Inga.

lil blue

Classic campervan ownership seldom stops at just the one and owner Allan couldn't help himself when this Dormobile Roma MKII crossed his path.

'While I was the Dormobile Owners' Club secretary, I was informed by a member that a rusty Roma was available to anyone for a charitable donation. The one stipulation was that it needed to be collected within two weeks or it was destined for the scrap heap.'

No one else was able to mobilize themselves within the time limit, so Allan stepped in. 'Once in my possession it sat for a further year in dry storage before I embarked on the restoration. It took four years to complete and I gave myself a deadline for displaying it at a local classic car show.'

'The interior only needed a few coats of varnish to bring it back to life; amazing considering how bad the exterior was.'

'We had no intention of getting another camper but the rarity value of this Roma persuaded me otherwise. Brenda, my wife, is not keen on sleeping in the Roma so we tend to use it instead for days out.'

'The original owner kept a log and diary of all aspects of the camper, from fuel economy and mileage to oil levels; so out of respect to his dedication I have kept this tradition going.'

style notes

This 1968 micro-camper is a conversion by Dormobile. The van features a reduced-scale version of the archetypal striped rising roof. There is also a pramback fixed to a drop-down tailgate. Small is beautiful in the case of Lil Blue.

The seats fold down to make a double bed and a child's sling-type bunk was designed to be fitted into the roof. This van still has the original curtains, which are fixed all around the interior, including the windscreen. A single-ring swing-out cooker and a small foldaway sink that drains to the outside via a small pipe means that simple one-pan meals can be prepared.

Maybe it's the combination of the pale blue exterior with cream flash with the red and white stripy roof, maybe it's the novelty of being able to fit so much into such a small space, but it has to be said, this camper has charm.

Very few of these are still in roadworthy condition: if you see one you are in for a treat.

'I've been into classic VWs since I was a teenager and have owned 1964 and 1954 Beetles. The latter was a £165 wreck, bought and restored over three years, becoming a prize-winning car. I kept that for 20 years until I swapped it for another wreck, a 1960 Porsche 356B which I'm currently restoring.'

southend

'I bought this VW T2 because I couldn't wait for the Porsche to be ready – like an impetuous child I wanted a toy for the summer,' recalls owner Phil. 'I have always fancied a camper. Originally I hankered after a split screen rather than a bay window, but when I saw this one for sale I simply couldn't get over its amazing original condition – I just had to buy it before someone else did.'

'The previous owner had bought it for his birthday. Being a university lecturer he had long holidays, so he celebrated his fortieth with a tour of the Alps. The camper didn't miss a beat for the whole 6000-mile trip – impressive for a vehicle of this age.'

'It was a great find and a great addition to the family: my three children, Oscar, Saffron and Finn, all love it and clamour to go out in it rather than in our modern cars.'

style notes

The cool combination of the immaculate white bodywork, including painted bumpers and wing mirrors, and the amazing showroom condition means that this vehicle attracts attention wherever it goes.

Built in 1972 and stored in a container on a merchant ship for two years before it was registered proved to be a good start for this particular VW. All its subsequent owners have lavished equal care and attention on the vehicle.

The current owners use it for local days out and on longer trips to the countryside – longer being the operative word as speed is not what this van is about.

It is an elegant and restrained example of a perfect bay-windowed VW T2. Nothing has been altered, and little has been added, apart from some beach towels to clean up sandy feet and a few favourite toys to keep the children occupied.

The uncluttered, vanilla-toned original interior is perfectly in keeping with the exterior. It is as joyous to be in as to look at. Both inside and outside this van is a visual feast.

weird and wonderful

From a converted French fire truck to an 'extension' to a regular saloon car, these campers are the customized, the idiosyncratic and the unusual.

While some campervans are mass produced, or created by smaller conversion companies, others are one-offs that reflect the imaginations of their owners. These distinctive vehicles have been created to provide space and headroom so that their owners can comfortably stand up, cook and sleep in them.

Individual and unusual, these campers combine imaginative thinking with new materials and new technologies. The development of fibreglass or GRP (glass-reinforced plastic) during World War II later found its way into vehicle design, allowing curved areas to be created within the context of the traditional coach-built (square) bodywork.

While some of these vehicles are visually more successful than others, there is no lack of lateral thinking and ingenious ideas in their conception and construction. These campers are inspiring and thought provoking.

ginetta car-camper

'First prize in the "most unusual design" category!' jokes Arthur, owner of this one-of-a-kind car-camper.

In the late 1960s, kit car manufacturer Ginetta – 'masters of fibreglass' – dipped their toes into building campervans. Unfortunately the idea was short-lived and only one was made. The camper was stored in the company's factory for a few years until a group of mechanics and racing drivers decided to use it for accommodation when motor racing.

'A relocation of the factory forced the sale of the camper, but it was not restored. A friend of mine purchased it years later, by which time it was in a pretty sorry state and needed a major restoration,' explains Arthur.

'Now it's in my possession it gets well used. I'm not one for manicured campsites, I prefer 'wild camping'. It's more of an adventure to stop whenever and wherever it takes my fancy – and cheaper, too.'

'It certainly attracts attention – double takes and rubbernecking are a regular occurrence. I am proud to own it and display it at classic car shows: something as unusual as this needs to be shared with others.'

'I plan to take an extended holiday to Europe with the Ginetta, to indulge my hobby of metal detecting. Maybe I'll find my fortune...but I'll still keep the camper.'

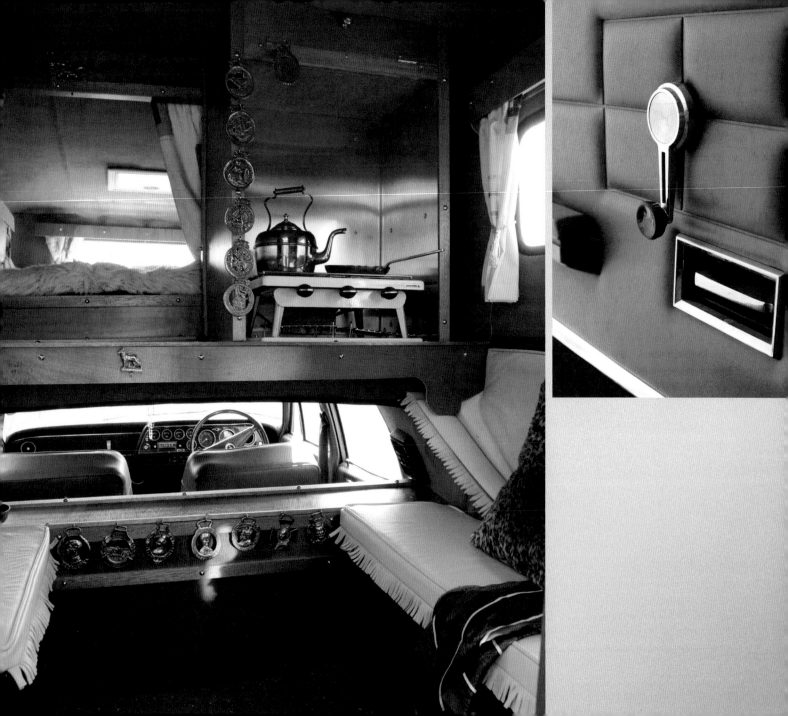

style notes

This campervan was designed to say 'modern', 'creative', 'top of our game' and 'look at me!'

It is a unique vehicle, based on a 1970s' Ford Zodiac executive saloon fitted with a walnut dashboard and plenty of eye-catching instrumentation.

The custom-moulded fibreglass campervan addition provides a snug sleeping area, a small cooker and a sitting area with striking white leather upholstery.

Stylistically the fibreglass exterior has echoes of yacht design with its sleek, sweeping lines. The interior is lined with wood veneer and conjures up an image of a narrow boat cabin.

Although it is a one-off, and a somewhat strange-looking one, this car-camper certainly celebrates technical and creative originality.

debbie

'I first saw this camper when I was in my early twenties, when I visited the Earls Court Motor Show in London. I remember thinking just how stylish and ahead of its time it was,' recalls Allan.

'Move forward 20 years when marriage, family, jobs and houses took priority. Then, in the late 1980s, I saw one parked in a lay-by and it sparked my interest. Several weeks later I saw yet another and I knew it was a sign that I had to have one!'

Allan looked in the magazine *Exchange and Mart* to see if there were any for sale, but drew a blank, so instead he advertised. 'I had three replies and went for the cheapest – a 1968 Bedford CA Dormobile Debonair – which has probably cost me more in the long run.'

The camper boasts a very practical layout as it has two living spaces, so the children can be tucked up in bed while the adults enjoy the evening.

'Over several years we worked on restoring her. At the time we owned a craft shop so Debbie came in very handy when towing our trailer to craft shows; she also doubled as a comfy place to sleep. We still take her to craft fairs and nowadays Debbie generates just as much interest as the crafts we are showing.'

style notes

The almost human face of the front of the Bedford Debonair, with its wide smile of radiator grille and indicator lights and headlights that look like big round eyes with protruding eyebrows, give the front of this vehicle instant appeal.

This is the only part of the vehicle that is metal. The rest of the body is made entirely of moulded fibreglass and was considered advanced for its day. It meant that curves could easily be incorporated into the shape and the paintwork colours cleverly bonded into the resin.

Other characteristic features of the Debonair are the deep curved side windows and the two smaller panes above the windscreen that not only help the driver's visibility but also add a sense of light and airiness to the interior.

It has the look and feel of a leisure vehicle; the colour of the bodywork and the window style mean it is frequently mistaken for an ice-cream van.

The interior was modern for its time, with smooth Formica and wood veneer surfaces and vinyl upholstery. It benefits from the addition of blankets and cushions to add texture and pattern, important details to consider if you are trying to create a homely feel. The driver's cab has the original Dormobile curtains in a 1960s' loose geometric design.

citroën h van

When Pierre Franchiset designed the Citroën H Van way back in 1947, with its distinctive corrugated sides for strength and economy over sleek good looks, little did he know just what an iconic vehicle he had created. Little was changed over its 34 years of production.

Over 473,000 were made, many of which have been adapted into various guises over the years.

Rob and Joyce were looking for a camper with a little more *je ne sais quoi* to replace their 1970s' VW pop-top; an H Van was on their wanted list.

'We spotted this ex-fire department 1972 H Van and it fitted the bill.' Now named Hetty, this quirky French camper has become a much-loved part of the family. 'It suited conversion to a campervan very well,' explains Rob. 'I spent a year making the cabinets while Joyce decorated. We left the original signwriting as it's a nice reminder of the vehicle's origin.'

'When we get away in Hetty it gives us a chance to relax and relish the atmosphere of a new location, in something different from your average camper.' Rob and Joyce like nothing better than a barbecue and a game of dominoes, which has become a ritual for every new destination.

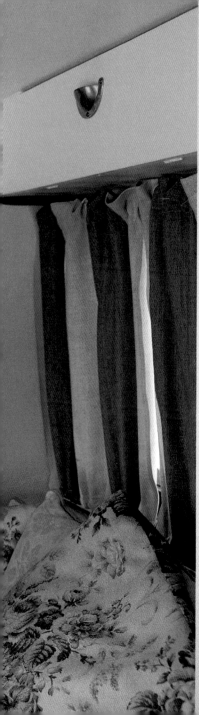

style notes

A reminder of the H Van's past life is emblazoned proudly on the side door, but there are other clues to its former use in the vehicle design, such as the flat windscreen, large door mirrors and the sliding doors to allow the firefighters to jump out quickly and easily.

The awning has been fashioned from a redundant fireman's hose, and other key features have been left intact in homage to the van's earlier life.

All the interior colours are in warm and light tones, which allows small decorative details to be added in complementary tones, and keeps a fresh and relaxing feel.

The reason why this vehicle is such a comfortable and satisfying space is because of the attention to detail and the immaculate finish throughout. Nothing here irritates or distracts.

bmc princess

Despite first impressions this camper is not a conversion. In fact it was coach-built, in 1967, on a Vanden Plas Princess chassis by J H Jennings, a company that was more used to working on Ford, Bedford and Commer chassis; this campervan is absolutely unique.

John Lunt became the very proud owner of this commanding vehicle in 1976 and has used it to tour Scotland and Europe with his wife, Geraldine.

'The camper was finished to exacting standards with materials like walnut and leather, more often found in limousines for dignitaries,' explains John. 'The original owner wanted nothing but the best. Many of the features of this camper were unheard of on similar campervans of the era, including power steering and an automatic transmission.'

'It attracts attention wherever we go, sometimes for the wrong reasons, as many Princesses still serve as either wedding cars or hearses.'

'The interior, although sizeable, is only designed for use by a couple. No room for a chauffeur, despite its pedigree,' laughs John.

Having had the camper for such a long time it is unlikely John will be looking to sell it anytime soon. After all, what could replace it?

style notes

Jennings was an established campervan conversion company in the north of England that used traditional coachbuilding techniques.

This vehicle features many of the manufacturer's signature design details, such as the curve of the moulded fibreglass roof and the sweeping contrasting colour flash running the full length of the vehicle. The storage area above the driver's cab is another typical Jennings feature.

Their interiors always follow a favoured format, with a living area separate from the two front seats and a wood-lined interior with facing bench style seating.

The overall feel is somewhat regal. The tones of the wood, turquoise furnishings and the elegant cream paintwork give the Princess an air of sophistication. It is easy to imagine her travelling along at a steady pace with her head held high.

'It all started back in mid-1970. I brought a VW, enjoyed it, sold it and bought a Bedford CF panel van. I fitted a high roof and windows and then, with the help of my wife, Valerie, we kitted it out to our liking,' explains Brian.

'An obsession was born. It carried on from there: Ford, Bedford, Austin, Morris and so on. I get most pleasure out of restoring them, though of course they are used on the occasional road trip.'

'While looking for my next project I saw Gerty, as she is known, advertised in a classic car magazine. I liked what I saw. Six months later she was advertised again, only a bit cheaper; I didn't need any further convincing.'

'Gerty started life as a saloon car. In the late 1970s the saloon body had rotted, so it was removed and replaced with a coach-built caravan body, based on a 1930s' Eccles motor caravan. The owner tinkered with it but lost interest, so it lay under canvas for 15 years.'

'When l got my hands on her the chassis had rusted – no brakes, no wiring, no engine. I worked on her every day (even Christmas) for two and half years. Unlike past projects I am reluctant to part with Gerty; maybe I've changed after all these years.'

morris oxford

style notes

The country cottage aesthetic runs deep, touching many people with feelings of comfort and security and images of a more relaxed and charming lifestyle.

The mock Tudor beams, warm-toned wood and comfortable deep-buttoned velvet upholstery – together with a traditional-style fabric of blown roses in pinks and creams, china cups, brass utensils and a copper kettle simmering on the stove – celebrate the rural idyll. The leaded light windows help to reinforce the theme.

The fact that this is a country cottage on wheels with a 1930s' vintage car up-front, panelled bodywork and a lantern roof make it even more convincing. All the driver needs to do is to ensure that they always find an idyllic spot in which to park!

american beauties

The large American Recreational Vehicles or RVs fulfil just about everyone's expectations of a comfortable life on the road. Built for a highway system that can happily accommodate them, and affordable petrol prices, RVs are ideal for making major journeys.

The imposing scale of the RV suits the big landscape and the wide-open spaces of the US. Inside, the RV's character is defined by quality materials, stately design and generous proportions, giving their owners a taste for the glamour of the great American road trip.

Many RVs are purpose-built. They incorporate degrees of comfort that are way beyond the notion of camping or making do: built-in bathrooms, thick pile carpet, lavish upholstery and carpentry are a particular feature of these RVs, along with full-size cookers, fridges and high-spec furnishings. This, together with the fact that many RVs only take to the road for an annual vacation, gives them an enviable lifespan.

The enduring appeal of the RV lies in its iconic design and long association with the romantic notion of the great road journey.

winnebago brave

'Believe it or not I was looking to purchase a log cabin, but somehow ended up with this behemoth of an American motorhome'.

'I'm not known for spending money on myself,' says Andy. 'I'll resist buying new shoes until the old pair has fallen apart, which makes my impulse purchase even more remarkable, causing shock and amusement among family and friends. One friend commented that most mid-life crises involve women or sports cars, but I ended up with this!'

Joking aside, Andy has no regrets, and the 1973 Winnebago Brave has turned out to be one of his better purchases. Andy continues: 'I can even overlook the fuel consumption that the warbling V8 engine demands: the fuel gauge moves like the second hand on a clock! So the big plans we had to travel to Provence are on hold for now – we prefer to travel around locally. As soon as I end up at my destination I feel as though I am a million miles away and can forget all my woes.'

'You tend to hear the Winnebago before seeing it. I find it rather amusing to see the reactions on people's faces as we thunder round the corner.'

'The front of the Winnebago looks like it's cheesed off, but it sure does make people smile.'

'Luckily it serves as a spare room too, which was the original intention with the log cabin!'

style notes

The striking appearance of the front of this Winnebago, with its chunky metallic features and angled split-screen windshield, is almost heroic. It certainly looks as though it means business.

Running the whole length of the sides of the van is the famous 'flying W' logo of Winnebago. It is a strong graphic shape; setting the red against the shiny metal was an inspired choice.

The Winnebago brand is named after a Native American tribe and the Brave is one of a series that also included the Chieftain and the Warrior. A previous owner picked up on this theme and fixed kitsch/romantic painted plates of Native Americans to the van's walls. The current owner initially tried to remove them, but found them so securely fixed he decided it was best to leave them there. Now the interior has a rough-edged American feel that perfectly suits its new coastal home of windswept and rugged beauty.

'My father took me on several trips to Belgium and Le Mans in his campervan and I loved every minute of it,' reminisces Graham. 'On one journey home my father clapped eyes on a sleek low GMC motorhome for sale at a garage: it was love at first sight. Despite the salesman's best attempts my father decided to give it a miss – something he later regretted.'

'Several years later a neighbour informed my father that a big American motorhome was parked up in a local lay-by. Curiosity got the better of him and he decided to investigate. By an amazing coincidence it turned out to be the same GMC motorhome. The owner was reluctantly selling the vehicle as his business was struggling. This time my father wasn't going to let the opportunity slip away.'

'My father became slightly obsessed by these amazing vehicles and started to collect others. Several were previously owned by racing car and superbike teams to accommodate stars of the 1970s such as Barry Sheene and Emerson Fittipaldi. Their choice of a GMC motorhome may be due in part to the fact that it holds, even to this day, the speed record for a motorhome.'

'My father has now passed on but I still have a strong loyalty to his collection. I plan to start travelling around Europe and particularly to my favourite destination, Portugal.'

gmc motorhome

style notes

This huge, heavy and fantastically glamorous 1976 motorhome has the look of a fully specified interior-designed bachelor pad from 1970s' Palm Beach.

It's a period that has found favour with today's interior designers. In this case the coordinating lime, yellow and cream textured upholstery of the full-size armchairs and seating at the rear, along with the lime bouclé driver's and front passenger's seats, give the interior a breezy elegance. The slatted teak-coloured cupboards and the thick pile lime green carpet give the whole a decidedly 1970s' ambience.

The swivel chairs can be positioned into conversation groups or as a more traditional face-to-face layout.

The driver's seat also swivels, and is reminiscent of the interior of an executive jet or a sci-fi spaceship. From the outset GMC designed the vehicle with the intention of creating something new, a motorhome as a means of comfortable and luxurious travel, rather than as a vehicle fitted with the basics for camping.

dodge xplorer 21

This 1968 Dodge Xplorer made its way to England with the help of the United States Air Force: a serviceman brought it over when he relocated. 'He was a big fan of the British Mini, so his plan was to use the campervan as accommodation and tow vehicle so he could attend classic car shows,' explains Terry, the current owner.

'Unfortunately he was unaware of the British MOT and since the Dodge required some work it remained on the airbase for three years.' Terry noticed the van deteriorating and tried unsuccessfully to purchase it.

Terry's passion for campervans started at an early age. 'In my twenties I toured Europe for five months in a Bedford van with only a mattress in the back for comfort; this was the first of many campervans over the years.'

'In 1993 the American government announced the closure of the airbase and the serviceman had to return to America. This helped me strike a deal to buy the Dodge; the airman purchased two Minis to take back home. Even though the campervan was in England it was technically on American soil, therefore, bizarrely, I had to go through the import procedure, albeit just the paperwork.'

The Dodge is extremely well used by Terry and his wife Pauline, who regularly travel around England and France. 'We've been away on many trips with our children and our love of campervans has influenced them too: they both now own VW campervans.'

style notes

The common challenge in converting a van into a campervan is how to provide sufficient headroom. The designers of this Dodge campervan came up with some clever solutions. Additional headroom has been created by lowering the floor section of the van from the door to the seating/dining area. Positioning the cooker just off this dropped floorwell allows the 'chef' to cook in comfort.

The original van before conversion would have had two rear doors, but the back of the van now houses the bed. A single side door was fashioned from the original rear doors.

The van suits the outdoor lifestyle of its owners. There's space to transport bicycles; surfboards go on the roof rack. It doesn't pander to fashion or trends: its sturdy upholstery and fittings provide a no-nonsense and family-friendly campervan.

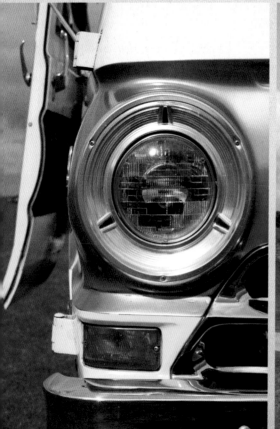

myrtle

'48 hours, two border crossings and a 1000-mile round trip from Calgary, Canada. But let's start at the beginning,' says Capri, the proud owner of this 1964 Dodge Travco motorhome.

'I came across Myrtle – aka Big Blue Fridge, due to the lack of heating – in Bozeman, Montana, in the autumn of 2007. I spent months keeping in contact with the owner, reassuring him I really was going to buy her as soon as all the paperwork was in order and when the snow had melted. In March 2008 we set off and made it all the way to Great Falls, Montana. Next day we completed the final leg of the journey and met the owner.'

'I can't adequately describe the feeling I had when I saw the old motorhome up close for the first time. Many months earlier the thought of owning a motorhome had never even crossed my mind. Now, however, common sense and environmental concerns were sidelined by the sheer beauty of this beast – all I wanted to do was get Myrtle home.'

'Fast forward nearly three years, many hours of labour and dollars later – it turns out Myrtle needed more work than we thought, but once you get started it's hard to stop.'

'With most of the work now complete we have focused on the styling, using only vintage items: linens, curtains, pots, dishes and decorations. She's not just a campervan, she's a mobile museum, a homage to the glorious "glamping" of yesteryear.'

style notes

The Dodge Travco, although built along aerodynamic lines, has a shape reminiscent of a coach, albeit in this instance with more charm and presence. It is in its element against big horizons and is perfectly suited to life on wide open roads. It has always been well regarded in terms of a quality build and respected for its longevity and toughness.

Myrtle's beauty, her stately proportions and full-scale fittings are much appreciated by her current owners, who have restored and refurbished the van with vintage items. The care with which these have been sourced is apparent – they look perfectly at home.

The design of the curtain fabric with its snowy peaks not only suits the scale and grandeur of Myrtle but also picks up on the exterior blue of the van and on a sunny day matches the blue skies beyond. It is a lovely stylized print, often seen on vintage travel labels and posters. The happy marriage of vintage items in the campervan setting is a credit to the owners.

airstream

'In my youth I was privileged to be the only chap in our group to possess a driving licence. Our usual weekend jaunts involved meeting at the local dance and then afterwards we would bundle into the works van and head for the coast. The van would then be our very primitive accommodation for the weekend,' explains Chuck Berry – not his real name, but a nickname that stuck.

'Roll on a few years – well, almost 30 – five caravans and three motorhomes later, but there was always the hankering for an American RV.'

A few more years went by before Chuck and Mary found a perfect example for sale in Texas. 'It transpired that the owner bought the motorhome only about eight months earlier but never used it. After some haggling we purchased this very nice 1983 Airstream motorhome – 'Baby', as I call her.'

The Airstream left its desert home and started its long journey. First south to Galveston, dodging the hurricanes on the way, then unceremoniously dumped in the hold of a ship bound for Europe.

'She arrived at Southampton safely after several weeks at sea, looking very tired and dirty. Quite a shock from when I last saw her gleaming in the Texas sunshine. So there you are, from works van to Airstream in a few long steps.'

style notes

This Airstream motorhome has a large open-plan living space, kitchen with all mod cons and full-size fittings. It celebrates the 1980s' American dream home with its luxurious thick pink carpet, coordinating vinyl and velour seating and walnut effect veneer finishes. This sense of luxury continues through to the bedroom: the wardrobes are fully lined with cedarwood to deter moths.

Airstream was clearly influenced by the very best from aerospace design. The overhead sliding cupboards reference the overhead lockers above aircraft seats.

This is a light, roomy and warm-toned space where even the tortoiseshell perspex and gold clock is in harmony with the interior. The retro bargello fringed cushions and the dream catcher add to its charm.

classics

In terms of production and popularity, some vehicle designs last longer than others. The VW T2 campervan is, without doubt, the front runner. This iconic vehicle, first introduced 60 years ago, remains the best-known campervan. Models have changed over the years: our featured model is from the first generation of T2s, with the distinctive split windscreen.

During the 1960s and early 70s, British motor industry was more focused on its home markets. Long-established production techniques and traditional materials produced a string of classic panel vans, such as the Ford Transit, the Commer and the Bedford. In the UK it was left to small enterprises and designers to convert these landmark vehicles into campervans. Relying on the materials of the moment – such as Formica and fibreglass (glass-reinforced plastic) – and their own ingenuity, these early entrepreneurs created their own masterpieces, building in pop-top roofs, galley-style kitchens and clever systems for converting seating into beds. Some companies' conversions were more successful and enduring than others.

The examples in this chapter are campervan conversions based on vehicles that started life as panel vans. They provide an intriguing insight into the early days of the classic campervan. Each one featured here is still on the road, and each demonstrates a striking sense of quality and design.

wildgoose mini

'Our passion for campervans began after the birth of our daughter, Jennifer,' says Rob. 'As an ex-Scout I felt at home under canvas, but my wife Audrey was not so keen. A compromise was reached: a 1973 Commer Haylett PB campervan.'

'While thumbing through a car magazine I saw an article about a Wildgoose Mini campervan – and so began my quest to find one.' Between 1963 and 1968, 62 were said to have been made, of which around a dozen survived, half abroad and possibly three on the road in England. It took Rob several years before he tracked down one for sale.

'I drove to meet the reluctant vendor, who showed me a tired but basically sound Wildgoose. I made an offer and after an anxious week the deal was done. I started a complete restoration, which took four years.'

'Restoration was completed in time for a trip to Holland with the Classic Camper Club. Car horns honking and people photographing us was a regular occurrence during the trip.'

'On one trip to Worthing we visited the original designer, Ted Bennett, an elderly gentleman in his eighties. Unfortunately the "goose" didn't make him a millionaire, but he and his wife were delighted we took the time to visit.'

'Our Wildgoose is a Popular Plus, 3+1 berth with optional hammock making 4+1 – yes, five sleeping in a Mini!'

style notes

Converted from a basic British Motor Corporation (BMC) Mini van, these extraordinary-looking and creative conversions were carried out by a small independent British company. Some key features of Minis of the 1960s include the sliding driver and passenger windows and the cord-pull interior door handles. The rear addition was made using traditional coachbuilding techniques. Though clearly recognizable as a Mini, the van appears to have morphed into a birdlike shape with a curved storage unit above the cab, hinged raising roof and stylized sloping side windows.

The upholstery is original, a dense and hard-wearing textural moquette with a small geometric pattern.

This owner has a collection of original eight-track tapes from the mid-1960s and 70s: the Beatles, T Rex and the Four Tops. He has sourced driving gloves in the style of the day and has a fabulous period picnic hamper, a much treasured family heirloom whose colours work well with the colours of the van.

Wildgoose may be small, but is well preserved and much loved.

a pair of commers

To say that Martin is a fan of Commer van conversions is a huge understatement.

'My collection now numbers more than 20 vehicles. The first Commer I bought was an old TV detector van. This was followed shortly afterwards by a Post Office van and a minibus. In recent years I have acquired a butcher's van, an ambulance, a pick-up, a fire engine, a Telecom van and the odd campervan.'

'The first camper was a very rare 1962 Hadrian PA conversion. The seats had tapestry fabric that depicted various European characters such as bullfighters. Sadly, as it had been used for a number of years as a static caravan on the cliff tops of Whitby, it was in poor condition.'

'The last van we purchased is the Hadrian you see here on pages 100–101, 'Rosie'. It had no rust at all and had been owned by one family since its manufacture. Apparently this was the last Hadrian to be built. When the original family were looking to buy, they went to various dealers and insisted on sleeping one night in all the vans they were interested in, finally choosing the Hadrian as the best. So far we have used this one for a couple of weekends and agree with the original purchasers – this is most definitely our favourite.'

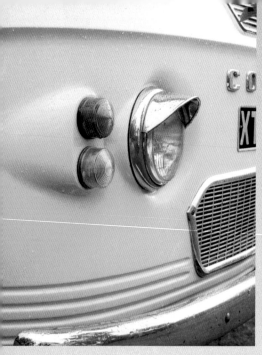

style notes

Commers were popular vehicles for conversion into campervans. The van on the previous pages was converted by Hadrian, a company based in Northumberland that took its name from the nearby Hadrian's Wall. The company produced this particular model for five years, from the early to mid-1960s.

The delightful sweep along the side and back of this Commer immediately conveys a sense of leisure time and holidays; it is a nostalgic organic shape reminiscent of ice-cream vans. The sweep is outlined in aluminium trim against the pale blue and cream of the coachwork. It adds an almost feminine touch to an otherwise quite heavy and boxy-shaped vehicle.

The interior, lined with oak veneer, was based on the inside of a touring caravan of the period. The kitchen is positioned at the back of the van beneath the louvred window and has a domestic feel about it, in the same way that a kitchen sink at home works best when there is a view.

The yellow Commer on these pages was converted by Clearway, a company from West Yorkshire. The van has been refurbished with a cheery lemon yellow vinyl that coordinates with the exterior.

Good design and quality internal fitments give these vans their classic status.

land rover dormobile

'When I started looking for a Land Rover I had just started kite buggying. Living on the outskirts of London didn't give much scope for strapping yourself into a three-wheeled buggy, launching a 6-metre wide kite and hurtling along at 30 mph. So I needed a vehicle in which I could carry the kit and stay away for a night or two,' explains John.

'Advertised locally was a Land Rover Dormobile. I had never heard of these, but it seemed perfect, a deal was done and 'Leaky' was mine. Searching the internet I found two clubs that look after owners with this type of vehicle: the Dormobile Owners' Club, of which I'm now Chairman, and the Series 2 Club.'

'One of the main club events is the annual London to Brighton run which takes place every October, when 1000 old Land Rovers shake, rattle and roll their way between Crystal Palace and Brighton for a fun day out. Unfortunately my Land Rover leaks, hence its name – oil leaks out and rain leaks in.'

'It truly is a multi-purpose vehicle and performs faultlessly in snow, pulling other cars up hills and getting me to work whatever the weather.'

style notes

The legendary Land Rover, built for strength not beauty, could be considered an incongruous choice for a campervan. This conversion by Dormobile has created a vehicle easily suited for a tough four-wheel drive lifestyle but which also meets John's basic weekend needs. It acts as a 'base camp', somewhere to shelter from the rain, change out of muddy boots and have a brew-up.

The simplicity and highly functional design, with sturdy metal cabinetry and rubber mats, mean that mud and mess can easily be washed down.

The interior is kitted out in practical materials without losing its own aesthetic. Vintage 100% wool blankets, celebrating the beauty of natural tones, some tin mugs and a kettle – all you need is a campfire. And best of all you can get to the places a standard campervan can't hope to access.

'I've always preferred vans to cars: they seem more reliable, stronger and adaptable – one minute you're loading a van with furniture, the next with mates. I was about 25 when I saw an advert for a 1964 Bedford CA Dormobile Romany. I went to have a look, and although it wasn't very pretty, I bought it as I could see the potential.'

bedford ca

For many years Tony travelled with his companion, Doreen. After numerous trips in the Bedford over the years, they decided that they needed something more comfortable, so they purchased a modern campervan. 'I couldn't bear to sell my trusty CA so I parked it in the back garden, but after a couple of years Doreen nagged me to get rid of it.'

'While working in Germany I phoned home and was told someone was there buying my CA. Sadly I wasn't there to say goodbye.'

'Doreen's grandson, Dennis, decided he wanted a CA as he had happy childhood memories of holidays in mine. We made enquiries and found a suitable one for sale, which he purchased.'

'Dennis was going to be married and managed to convince his wife-to-be that it would make a great wedding car. It looked fantastic – as did the bride.'

'He kept it for about a year before opting to sell it. I decided to buy it as it reminded me of Doreen, who by this time had passed away. It brought back many happy memories and funny moments that we had shared together.'

style notes

The Bedford CA was a popular commercial vehicle which proved equally popular as a campervan conversion.

This model by Dormobile sports the characteristic striped vinyl rising roof. The matching pale green bodywork with contrasting white flash and bonnet lends an airy feel, especially with the roof up. It was delivered with good-quality fittings such as the cooker, sink and Easycool cool box and was designed to be 'ready to go'.

If a van has its own style or makes a strong design statement then only minor touches are needed to add tonal variation or interest. The palette here is restrained, with the beach towel and Welsh blanket chosen to complement the existing background.

ford road ranger

'Craig was not at all keen when I suggested a campervan. "I don't want anything I can't stand up in," was his response,' explains Marion. 'However, while I was away visiting my sister in America in June 1980, he saw 'Emmy', a Jennings Ford Road Ranger, for sale in a local garage and as she met the all important height criteria he bought her, without telling me.'

'On my return I did not take kindly to being whisked off to the workshop on the pretext of a work issue, but when I saw what was inside all was forgiven. She looked brand new despite being eight years old. The original owners had never used her so she only had delivery mileage on the clock. What a find!'

'We've enjoyed many holidays and weekends in her over the years. We used to have two dogs and, like us, they loved to walk. We would leave Emmy in the morning after we'd had a full English breakfast, and armed with map and compass would do a round trip that got us back to the van in time for me to cook an evening meal. All four of us weary but happy.'

'Emmy reminds me of a favourite auntie: she is reliable, welcoming, comfortable, a pleasure to stay with and we love her.'

style notes

This is based on the classic Ford Transit, a popular base vehicle for campervan conversion. Our featured example was converted by Jennings, based in Cheshire. It has the firm's signature design style that we can also see in the BMC Princess on page 68. The flash along the exterior, the curved roof and the internal layout are all very similar.

The coach-built body is aluminium over a wooden frame. Considered modern in its day, the Ford Transit added chrome details to headlights and hub caps. The American style influence is also seen in the small rounded ribs around the side of the front wings.

The rear door is reminiscent of the slam door of an old-fashioned railway carriage, with a sliding window; it is heavy and closes with a satisfying 'clunk'.

The quality fittings – wood lining and fabric upholstered seating – give the interior a classic feel and have clearly been designed to withstand the ravages of time. The owners have added a few home comforts such as a thick carpet. They clearly treasure and respect this favoured 'auntie' – shoes are left by the back door!

morris marina sun-tor

'I first met Mary one Christmas while at lodgings in the Lake District,' explains Eric. 'We were both there because we love outdoor life; a walking holiday, in what has now become our special place, was the perfect antidote to a commercial Christmas. We clicked and eight months later we got married.'

'We both preferred the freedom of self-catering holidays: doing things on our own terms, no fixed meal times, no missing breakfast because you overslept! So instead of jetting off abroad for our honeymoon we hired a campervan and toured Scotland.'

Campervan life suited Eric and Mary well, so early on in their marriage they purchased what has now become an icon of the 1970s, a 1977 Morris Marina Sun-Tor. 'We picked it up on Valentine's Day 1979 and have been the proud owners ever since.'

'The Marina is small and cosy but you adapt quickly. With it being a standard car size it's the perfect vehicle to escape in on a whim. As my wife is shorter than me she has kindly opted for the bed behind the steering wheel.'

'We've been all around the UK – to the back of beyond. We are both now in our senior years but we still make good use of the camper, even during the winter! And we like nothing better than taking a trip to the Lake District, to the place where we first met.'

style notes

This conversion of a Morris Marina panel van by Sun-Tor – based in Devon in the south of England – is recognizable by the distinctive design of the pop-top roof. No striped vinyl, just a clean warm white, with a shaped fibreglass cap that helps keep it waterproof. This is a vehicle that can function as a normal family car and be transformed into a campervan when required.

Unbelievably cosy and jam-packed with a cooker, sink, cupboards, and seats that fold down to form a double bed, the design of this small camper perfectly suits the lifestyle of its owners. They know how to make the most of the space and over time have developed their favourite campervan recipes, too.

The wood veneer cupboards, warm russet upholstery and original 1970s' brown, russet and yellow patterned print curtains all serve to create a warm and welcoming space. Parked up in a sunny spot, it would be the perfect refuge for an afternoon nap.

vw westfalia campmobile

'It was a combination of seeing a field of VW campervans and my own impending fortieth birthday that gave me the drive, excuse the pun, to want my own VW,' recalls owner Ian.

'It was a big purchase to justify, even for my birthday, and I had to convince my fiancée, Claire, that it was not just a fad, but something we could both enjoy.'

'While looking through a magazine I saw an article about a campervan that the owner had shipped from America before embarking on a three-year restoration. Why couldn't I do the same? This idea did not sit well with Claire, who accused me of having a mid-life crisis.'

'Eventually I found the perfect restoration project: my dream 1967 VW SO 42 Westfalia Campmobile. Initially the seller informed me it was sold, but luckily a few weeks later he contacted me as the sale had fallen through. We struck a deal and got 'Florence', as she is now called, shipped over to England.'

'With the help of my friend, an expert restorer, we got started on the mammoth four-year task of getting her to her current condition.'

'It has been an interesting journey, I have gained a lot of knowledge, met many happy-go-lucky enthusiasts and won awards at VW shows. But above all I have used her for what she was designed for...camping with a few home comforts thrown in.'

style notes

Westfalia was a German conversion company subcontracted by Volkswagen to convert some of its vehicles to campervans.

Florence, featured here, is one of the archetypal VW Type 2 split-screen vehicles that were produced between 1950 and 1967. The SO 42 is one of a series of SO special models produced by Westfalia.

There are a number of reasons why this van looks so dignified: white-wall tyres, white bumpers, top half and roof all make it special. In addition, the bodywork is immaculate. The hinged double doors create a feeling of openness that is very engaging and goes a long way towards explaining the perennial appeal of the VW Type 2 campervan.

The interior is birch lined and the upholstery is black vinyl. The small pop-top provides standing height over the main living and seating areas and the louvred windows with fly screens show the attention to detail that Westfalia expended on its conversions.

Elegant, classic and well loved, this is a beautiful example of the VW T2.

new retro

Collections, obsessions, interests and hobbies can lend a visual to styling, and these campervans amply illustrate this. They reflect their owner's unique styles and interests. The vehicles can function as an artist's workroom or as a photographer's studio...and offer a different view every day.

Despite the compact internal spaces of these campers, creative owners have been able to make their mark on their vans and to take to the road for further inspiration. These are not only places to camp out or chill out, they are happy extensions of creative lives.

What characterizes the new retro campervans are the items that have been acquired, inherited or re-purposed; collections that have been put together in a planned and stylish way.

While the results may look fashionable, this is not the end game. These campervans are stylish by default.

vw devon This 1978 VW Devon campervan, owned by Anthony since 1997, has successfully completed many a long-distance European trip.

'As a family we had been camping for many years, but the time came for a four-wheeled upgrade,' says Anthony. 'The romance of owning a VW appealed but, frustratingly, the campervans I found in classified adverts were either sold before I had a chance to view or too big a project to make roadworthy. After six months of searching I had almost given up when by chance, on a journey home, I saw a VW for sale. I made a hasty U-turn, parked, hot-footed it up the driveway and knocked on the door to enquire. It was perfect so I bought it immediately.'

Anthony and his wife Hatty's first trip was to Spain with their four children, one of whom is this book's photographer, Tina. The trip was a success so bolder trips were notched up over the years, including a tour of Greece and an exhilarating journey over the Alps. 'My wife is a talented artist,' adds Anthony, 'so now the children have flown the nest the VW is finding a new use as a mobile art studio. We travel to remote parts of England, Scotland and Wales so that Hatty can paint the beautiful landscapes.'

style notes

This camper was created by Devon, a company based in Sidmouth, south-west England, who used this style for a lot of conversions in the 1970s. The pop-top roof in brown, mustard and white horizontal stripes is one of the company's signature features.

The restored exterior is in near-perfect condition, and the big sliding door, large expanse of glass, the steel sink and white cupboards all help to create a fresh, crisp feel. It is an inspirational space.

Family holidays inevitably change as children grow up and flee the nest, and the fundamental adaptability of the VW campervan is illustrated here. Having seen a multitude of family trips this gorgeous camper is now used as a means for the creative owners to travel and take their hobbies and interests with them, finding inspiration wherever they roam.

Watercolour and sketching materials are not bulky to carry and so can easily be stored until the moment is right for creativity. An unexpected view or object can spark the creative process.

morris a60 sun-tor

'As a young lad, every now and then on my walk to school I would see one of these vans parked outside a neighbour's house. I remember thinking how great it was. One day I peeked inside and knew that I would love to own one – when I could drive,' reminisces Ian.

'Back in 1999 a friend mentioned that a local car dealer had a 1969 Morris Sun-Tor for sale; I went to see it and purchased it straight away.'

'It was built as a campervan from the start and based on a highly adaptable chassis from the early 1950s.'

'It took six months of solid work (six days a week, nine hours a day) to restore. There wasn't much that I had to 'undo', it just needed bringing back into shape.'

'I love vintage things; I don't have much time for the modern stuff with all the techno wizardry and environmentally unfriendly plastics. I appreciate the quality and workmanship of yesteryear when things were built to last; nowadays we have such a throwaway culture.'

'Whether it's camping or attending classic car shows the Morris goes the distance with no problems. It will most likely outlive many of its modern counterparts.'

style notes

There is a striking sense of style about this vehicle, from the large area of glass to the immaculate paintwork in 'snowbird white', which perfectly matches the rising roof. It has a calmness that lets you appreciate the vehicle as a whole, with nothing to distract you from the beauty of the line. It is of museum quality.

The conversion is by Sun-Tor, a company with a well-deserved reputation for the high standard of its work. The interior layout is small but well designed and Sun-Tor has managed to fit a lot of essentials into a limited space.

The vehicle has two rows of seats, upholstered in dark cherry, a small wardrobe and a two-ring cooker with grill and sink concealed by a fold-down surface. It illustrates the virtues of good design and construction. Fortunately its owner has the passion and the talent necessary to restore items of true vintage quality. There is no need to fill this campervan with retro accessories; it carries its own visual weight.

clary

'My love of J2s came about when my father purchased a 1959 Austin 152 minibus. It took him all over the country when he worked away. Later in my life I owned a 1962 Morris J2 minibus with a fetching cream and pink exterior. This was followed by 'Clary', my 1961 Austin 152 car-camper, one of the only configurations of this type left,' explains Mick.

'She was in terrible condition – almost ready for the scrapyard! The previous owner said if I could get her restored for the following year she would be shown at the NEC Classic Car Show; a deadline is just what you need to focus the mind. I got it finished just in time and the many positive comments I received made all the hard work I had put in very worth while.'

'I've done most of the work myself, even though I am not that mechanically minded, but I have good family and friends who helped me along the way.'

'Another previous owner recounted the problems they had experienced with Clary overheating while touring Devon and Cornwall. Apparently when they reached the top of the infamous Porlock Hill they had a celebratory picnic to mark the occasion!'

'There is something you cannot fail to like about J2s, they are so full of character. We hope Clary goes on for ever: she is about to celebrate her half century.'

style notes

This very rare 1961 restored campervan has a striking curvy jelly-mould shape; the wood-lined interior has a warm and comfortable feel. Inside, the style is 1950s domestic and the chequerboard floor adds to this theme. The use of colour and retro-style patterns in reds, yellows, browns and greens continues the feeling of warmth and nostalgia that particularly suits this vehicle. It is a design that is equally suited to modern sensibilities.

The space is simple, with a one-piece rear door, a small kitchen and wardrobe, and a table and chairs that convert into a clever bed arrangement with a mattress that sits into the floor.

The front seats are removable and can be used as outdoor chairs too...a clever feature for a picnic with a touch of comfort.

mr baldwin

'Having owned a 1979 VW van for 11 years, I certainly had the bug, but longed for something older. We placed a "wanted" advert for our dream camper then sat back and waited,' explains Stuart.

'One afternoon in March 1997, my wife, Teresa, and I took a train to meet Mr Baldwin, who had replied to our advert. The 1965 Microbus with Devon Caravette interior that he was selling after 27 years sounded perfect. He met us at the station in the camper and I drove the short distance from the station to his house. Everything felt right and I was already grinning from ear to ear!'

'Mr Baldwin explained that, at the age of 77, his camping days were over. His grown-up children had very fond memories of their childhood holidays but weren't prepared to take the camper on, so he had made the tough decision to pass the van on to someone who would look after it and not paint it "silly colours". We had mixed emotions as we pulled away, happy and excited about our new camper, but slightly sad imagining how Mr Baldwin must have felt.'

'It's important to us to keep the camper as original as we can to preserve its integrity. I am a fan of mid-century design so I soon began to collect vintage accessories.'

'We have had some great holidays in the camper. We are always surprised how, after just a couple of days away, our camper feels like home.'

style notes

The owners of this immaculate split-screen VW expound the virtues of living the vintage lifestyle. Their collection of vintage camping wares is carefully and artfully selected. It is a vast collection, yet it maintains its integrity.

Vintage travel pennants are fascinating items, both in terms of travel memorabilia and as examples of graphic design. Their symmetry, shape and simple block colour designs look great as individual items and as a collection overall – a sort of retro bunting. They provide an interesting peek into the changing fashions of holiday destinations – Innsbruck, Cortina, Bavaria – stylish souvenirs of road trips past.

For these owners the word 'vintage' does not mean something kept in a glass case, but something to be used and enjoyed for everyday pleasure.

fiat 238 weinsberg

'I'd thought about buying a camper for ages and finally went for a 1978 VW Devon. It looked great but my love affair with the VW was crushed by the harsh reality of repeated mechanical failure, so I set about looking for a potential replacement.'

1970s' Fiats hold a particular fascination for Chris, who had owned a 128 1100 Special that he had bought in 2000, sold in 2003 and after much detective work bought back again in 2009.

'For months I had trawled the internet and eventually found a 1978 Fiat 238 Weinsberg for sale in Germany. It looked pretty good so I emailed the seller, who was kind enough to call me the next day. We struck a deal and I booked a flight to Frankfurt!'

'The seller met me, in the Fiat, at the airport. Halfway back to his home he pulled over and invited me to take the wheel. As I drove, he leaned over his seat, gazing into the rear of the van; I'm sure I detected a little moistening around his eyes. He'd owned the van for 12 years but he and his wife needed a few more comforts as they got older.'

'I use it most weekends in the UK and for the occasional longer trip in Europe. Eventually I plan to visit the old Fiat factory in Turin, which has a test track on the roof. A lap in the van would be just perfect – followed by an espresso, of course.'

'It's a testament to the former owner that it's never given me a moment's trouble. I'm utterly besotted with it and plan on keeping it well into my dotage.'

style notes

This vehicle has a similar driving position to the VW, where the driver sits over the front wheels. We also see hinged double doors at the sides of the van.

The double doors at the back mean that the seating area can easily become an al fresco dining room. The kitchen area is just inside the side doors, behind the driver's seat. A wonderful use of space, that integrates indoors and out by good design.

This is a convivial space to cook, to talk, to eat. Orange curtains and wood laminate table and kitchen worktops create a retro modern style, perfectly complemented by the typically 1970s' European tapestry pattern upholstery.

This lovely Fiat really has a timeless appeal.

cuthbert

'Our good friends are proud owners of a campervan called 'Margot' and the idea of owning one really appealed to us. Luckily we coerced our employer (the fashion label "Diesel") into purchasing a campervan for use as a promotional vehicle, as we are on the road for much of the summer,' explains Cat.

'We searched long and hard and eventually found a nice chap who specialized in vintage vehicles. He was selling a super-cool 1958 Bedford CA Dormobile split-screen, with fetching porthole windows, a slick paint job and a fabulous retro interior. Campervans of this pedigree rarely become available, so we purchased it without hesitation!'

En route to the Glastonbury Festival, Cat and Lucy collected 'Princess Cuthbert-Bunty Rose', as the Bedford is now called.

'We frequent many festivals and Cuthbert often sets up camp next to Margot – it's certainly an impressive sight. Most passers-by share a comment, give a thumbs-up or smile.'

When Cuthbert is not attending festivals his day job is to perform promotional duties for Diesel. 'We once covered Cuthbert in army surplus and drove around Buckingham Palace; we ended up being stopped seven times and asked what we were up to!' laughs Lucy.

style notes

This split-screen Bedford CA is the iconic campervan of its time. Bedford changed the design of its CA model from split-screen to one-piece windscreen in 1959: 'Cuthbert', from 1958, is one of the last models with this feature. It is easy to forget that when this vehicle was new, 13 years after World War II, food rationing in the UK had ended only four years earlier. This represented the ultimate leisure vehicle, designed to lift the spirits and encourage a feeling of optimism.

The turquoise and white livery, covered rear wheel arches, porthole windows and Dormobile roof all contribute to the sense of luxury – a valued commodity at the time the van was built.

Today, it again exudes optimism and joy. Its young owners enjoy their road trips, the conversations with neighbours at traffic lights, the summer festival life, and the fun of dressing the interior in a confident carefree way. Colours, textures and patterns are mixed. New and old accessories, fake flowers, picnic baskets and colourful textiles celebrate its cheerful style.

sourcebook

donna flower
Beautiful antique and vintage textiles. From 19th-century French fabrics to the vintage-inspired fabrics of today.
www.donnaflower.com

lucy bates vintage fabric
Fabrics from the golden age of British design.
110 High Street, Ashwell
Hertfordshire SG7 5NS
Tel: 01462 742905   www.lucybatesvintagefabric.co.uk

secondhand rose
Thousands of original vintage wallpaper and linoleum patterns.
230 5th Avenue suite No 510
New York, NY 10001, USA
Tel: 001 212 393 9002   www.secondhandrose.com

reprodepot
Reproductions of vintage and retro fabrics, for upholstery, dressmaking and crafts. Also dressmaking patterns and haberdashery.
www.reprodepot.com

fabrics galore
Ends of lines from designers and bargain finds for usual and unusual fabrics.
54 Lavender Hill
London SW11 5RH
www.fabricsgalore.co.uk

fine cell work
High quality needlepoint and embroidered cushions. A registered charity that teaches needlework to prison inmates and sells their work.
www.finecellwork.co.uk
Tel: 020 7931 9974

caravan
Quirky interiors shop, owned by interior stylist and author Emily Chalmers.
3 Redchurch Street, Shoreditch
London E2 7DJ   www.caravanstyle.com

hungerford arcade
Antiques centre with over 95 stallholders. Antiques and textiles in all price ranges. Good for a rummage.
26 High Street, Hungerford
Berkshire RG17 0NF
www.hungerfordarcade.co.uk

few and far
Beautiful old and new products, furniture, clothes, tableware, toys and crafts. Seasonally changing and very carefully chosen from artisans and producers around the world.
242 Brompton Road
London SW3 2BB
Tel: 020 7225 7070   www.fewandfar.net

the old cinema
Store devoted to antique, vintage and retro items.
160 Chiswick High Road
London W4 1PR
Tel: 020 8995 4166   www.theoldcinema.co.uk

pineapple retro
An eclectic mix of funky things dating from the 1950s to the 1980s.
Lyndhurst Road, Brockenhurst
Hampshire SO42 7RH
Tel: 07753 747297   www.pineappleicebucket.co.uk

luna
Specialists in 20th-century objects for the home.
139 Lower Parliament Street
Nottingham NG1 1EE
Tel: 0115 924 3267   www.luna-online.co.uk

circus
Always interesting shop, featuring individually sourced vintage homewares and fashion, and recycled and up-cycled items.
www.circus5thave.blogspot.com

linda bloomfield
Ceramicist making beautiful porcelain tableware in simple shapes with tactile satin matt glazes and coloured interiors.
www.lindabloomfield.co.uk

re
New and unique, unusual, recycled, reused and restored objects and textiles designed by Re and made locally whenever possible.
www.re-foundobjects.com

cox & cox
Exclusive range of home and outdoor accessories and gifts.
www.coxandcox.co.uk

pedlars
Vintage and modern homewares, including stylish camping equipment.
www.pedlars.co.uk

rockett st george
Imaginative and original homewares and gifts.
www.rockettstgeorge.co.uk

frasers aerospace
Suppliers of specialist, aerospace industry-approved cleaning and maintenance products. For metal polishing.
Tel: 020 8597 8781
www.frasersaerospace.com/metalpolishing.html

kp woodburning stoves
Affordable and individually crafted woodburning stoves.
Tel: 07764 813867   www.kpwoodburningstove.co.uk

deckchair stripes
Supplier by the metre of vintage-style striped cotton canvas for awnings, deckchairs and windbreaks.
www.deckchairstripes.com

leisure fayre
Suppliers of tent and awning poles, guy ropes and accessories.
www.leisurefayre.co.uk

outdoor world
Suppliers of metal-tipped wooden windbreak poles and other camping equipment.
www.outdoorworld.co.uk

vintage trailer supply
Suppliers of vintage-style awnings and accessories.
www.vintagetrailersupply.com

auto jumble – beaulieu
Huge annual event. Traders selling memorabilia, parts, accessories and vintage car and caravan finds.
www.internationalautojumble.co.uk

brent plastics
Plastic laminate sheeting in a multitude of styles and colours.
Unit D Cobbold Estate, Cobbold Road, Willesden
London NW10 9BP
Tel: 020 8451 0100   www.brentplastics.co.uk

the caravan club
Tel: 01342 326944 for general enquiries
Tel : 0800 328 6635 for membership enquiries
www.thecaravanclub.co.uk

classic camper club
Motorhome historian/writer Martin Watts founded the club in 1991 for owners of classic campervans and motorhomes.
www.classiccamperclub.co.uk

dormobile owners' club
Allan Horne, Secretary
www.dormobile.org.uk

tonke campers
www.tonkecampers.nl

torcars sun-tor register
www.brmmbrmm.com/torcars

yorkshire classic campers
Commer classic campers for holidays and film work. Also restoration and mechanical work on all types of classic campers.
www.yorkshireclassiccampers.co.uk

credits

We would like to thank all the owners for allowing us
to photograph their 'cool campervans'.

Endpapers photographed by Andrea McNamara.
All other photography by Tina Hillier unless otherwise stated.
www.tinahillier.com

old retro

simple life

weird and wonderful

american beauties

classics

new retro

acknowledgements

Jane Field-Lewis and Chris Haddon would like to thank everyone involved for their help in putting this book together.

A huge thank you to Pavilion Books and in particular our publisher Fiona Holman and our designer Georgina Hewitt for their continued support and help on this, our second book.

Our photographer Tina Hillier has worked tirelessly on this project and we are immensely grateful to her. As a child she had holidayed in campervans and this brought an added sensitivity to the project.

Thanks to our spouses, Robert and Emma, as well as other family and friends, for their continued help and support. Special thanks to Martin Watts and Pat McNamara for all their valued campervan advice.

It goes without saying that huge thanks go to the campervan owners who shared their stories with us and allowed us to photograph their much-loved vehicles.

jane field-lewis and chris haddon

Jane Field-Lewis is a London-based stylist working in film and photography. She co-owns a 1970s retro-modern styled caravan – a perfect little hideaway which inspires creativity. Chris Haddon has a passion for retro-caravanning and retro campervans and runs his design agency from a converted 1960s Airstream.

Additional captions: page 1 airstream; pages 2–3 ford road ranger; page 4 vw westfalia campmobile; page 6 morris marina sun-tor; page 9 citroën h van; pages 10–11 vw t25; pages 32–33 southend; pages 56–57 morris oxford; pages 72–73 myrtle; pages 94–95 bedford ca; pages 128–129 mr baldwin; page 160 vw devon

First published in the United Kingdom in 2011 by
Pavilion Books Company Limited
1 Gower Street
London WC1 6HD

www.pavilionbooks.com

Commissioning editor Fiona Holman
Photography by Tina Hillier
Styling by Jane Field-Lewis
Design Steve Russell
Editor Maggie Ramsay

A CIP catalogue record for this book is available from the British Library

ISBN 978-1-862-05905-4

10 9 8 7 6 5

Colour reproduction by Dot Gradations Ltd, UK
Printed and bound by GPS Group, Slovenia

This book can be ordered direct from the publisher at www.pavilionbooks.com